Three Unpublished Poems
By Louisa M. Alcott

" We sometimes hear of one who nearly died of a broken heart —
but Bronson Alcott nearly died of a broken dream."
— Mrs. Helen Bell

Fruitlands Collection

THREE UNPUBLISHED POEMS
By LOUISA M. ALCOTT

𝕱𝖗𝖚𝖎𝖙𝖑𝖆𝖓𝖉𝖘 𝕮𝖔𝖑𝖑𝖊𝖈𝖙𝖎𝖔𝖓

"We sometimes hear of one who nearly died of a broken
heart—but Bronson Alcott nearly died of a broken dream."
MRS. HELEN BELL

There is a room upstairs in the old house at Fruitlands in
Harvard, Massachusetts, where the visitors pause and look
about them with a softening glance and often with visible
emotion, as though they felt a sudden nearness to something
infinitely intimate and personal. They have come to see the
place where Bronson Alcott and the group of transcendentalists
cut themselves off from the world in the spring of 1843 and
tried to found a New Eden where Evil could find no entrance,
and where all might share in common the peace of an indus-
trious simple life, intermixed with study and close to the heart
of Nature; a spiritual and intellectual center where mind and
soul could grow in quiet seclusion, yet with sympathetic com-
panionship. This was Alcott's dream.

The comedy and tragedy of the experiment have been the
theme of many a magazine article, and years have come and
gone; yet hundreds of people cross the pastures to the lonely
spot each year, and wander through the house, and listen to
the story of the joy of the first glad, hopeful days and the
pitiful ending of this philosopher's plan for an earthly
Paradise.

There is so much that is quaint to see and seemingly im-
possible to hear, for there were some strange theories worked
out by this group of learned men, that a sudden outburst of
surprise and amusement will break into the recital of the tale;
but in the room upstairs they are wont to grow quiet and

speak in lowered voices, for they seem to feel the pathos there of the final disillusionment. It is the room where at the end of a laborious day Mrs. Alcott, with tired eyes, sewed and sewed, night after night, by the light of her one flickering lamp, and where Bronson Alcott, deserted by his followers, lay in his bed, with his face turned to the wall, and in his despair over the bitter failure of his most cherished dream, called upon death to release him.

The visitors stand and look at Mrs. Alcott's lace cap on the table by the window, and the little cuffs that fell over her busy, useful hands; at the sewing basket, left where she might have laid it when she was too wearied to thread another needle; at all the many personal things belonging to them both that speak so clearly of them and seem to bring them very near. And then they turn to read the manuscripts and letters that hang upon the walls; for on the walls at Fruitlands hang various original manuscripts that as yet have never been published, and among them are three poems by Louisa Alcott—Bronson Alcott's noted daughter. These are now put before the public for the first time, and surely they must stir a warm response in the most indifferent heart.

Indelibly impressed upon Louisa Alcott's memory were those days at Fruitlands, when her childish feet ran swiftly over the pastures and through the pine grove, and where in the early mornings she sat upon a granite boulder far up on the hill and "thought thoughts"—so her diary tells us. She afterwards was frequently heard to say that it was in those days at Fruitlands that the seeds of her literary talents were sown, which were to meet with such heartfelt appreciation from the reading public, and were to give such solace and comfort to the old age of her gifted father and devoted mother. Her love and reverence for her father and her pride in his attainments were very beautiful; and in order to appreciate what it was in him that inspired this great sentiment, not only in his daughter, but in so many leading men of that

time, the eccentricities of the man whom the world called unpractical and visionary must be forgotten, so as to get a glimpse of the Alcott who was the intimate friend of Emerson—a genius, a philosopher, an optimist, in spite of failure and in spite of opposition. Therefore it seems best to give some extracts from his own writings first that will reveal the tenor of his mind and the largeness of his heart and intellect, in order that the poems of the daughter may be more fully understood. The following extracts are from his book entitled "Tablets."

"If one's life is not worshipful," he writes, "no one cares for his professions. . . . We recognize goodness wherever we find it. 'Tis the same helpful influence beautifying the meanest as the greatest service by its manners, as if it did it not."

*   *   *   *   *   *   *   *   *

"Enthusiasm is existence; earnestness, life's exceeding great reward. . . .

"Our dispositions are the atmosphere we breathe, and we carry our climate and world in ourselves. Good humor, gay spirits, are the liberators, . . . the sure cure for spleen and melancholy . . . and he who smiles is never beyond redemption."

*   *   *   *   *   *   *   *   *

"The liberal mind is of no sect; it shows to sects their departure from the ideal standard, and thus maintains pure religion in the world. But there are those whose minds, like the pupil of the eye, contract as the light increases. 'Tis a poor egotism that sees only its own image reflected in its vision. . . . 'Only as thou beest it, thou seest it!' "

*   *   *   *   *   *   *   *   *

"One cannot be well read unless well seasoned in thought and experience. Life makes the man. And he must have lived in all his gifts and become acclimated herein to profit by his readings. Living at the breadth of Shakespeare, the depth of Plato, the height of Christ gives the mastery, . . . or if not that, a worthy discipleship."

And here is a quotation that reveals his great and beautiful love of Nature:

> "Nature is the good Baptist, plunging us in her Jordan streams to be purified of our stains and fulfil all righteousness. And wheresoever our lodge, there is but the thin casement between us and immensity. . . . Nature without, Mind within, inviting us forth into the solacing air, the blue ether, if we will but shake our sloth and cares aside and step forth into her great contentments."

These are enough to show the rarified atmosphere of his thought world. He lived upon the hilltops, so to speak. And it is curious to note that in spite of its derision, the world has come to value many of his ideas which at first were deemed but foolishness. The importance of taste and beauty in the schoolroom, for instance, is now accepted throughout the world. Yet when he first preached this, what was then a new idea, and had the walls of his Temple School in Boston tinted in restful colors, and placed the busts of Socrates and Plato and other learned philosophers where they could be looked upon with reverence by his pupils, it was thought to be absurd and even dangerous, for the old regime of ill-lighted, ill-ventilated schoolrooms, with bare, forbidding walls, was at its height.

So also with one of his much-laughed-at theories of farming. He advocated growing buckwheat and turning the crop back into the soil in order to enrich the land, and all the farmers threw their hands up as though he had lost his reason. Yet only a year ago, when the nations were at war, the Agricultural Department in Washington sent out bulletins urging farmers to do this very thing as an admirable and inexpensive method to pursue.

The fundamental principle of his dietary system was the exclusive use of fruits, vegetables, and all kinds of grain, eliminating all animal food. While this was carried to excess, the idea of it does not sound so very strange to modern ears,

Picture of Bronson Alcott's famous Temple School, Boston, Mass., where he taught his philosophy to young boys and girls. It was the first school to be decorated and furnished with artistic taste, and he believed it developed a sense of beauty and refinement. 1830–1834. The school was in the Masonic Temple.

there being plenty of vegetarians now to commend the theory. These things are mentioned in order to show that in spite of much that was wholly unpractical, he advocated many theories that have not died, but have taken root.

It was the intuitive consciousness of the sincerity of his appeal to the world that drew his daughter Louisa so closely to him and led her to express herself so touchingly in the following poems:

A. B. A.

Lines Written by Louisa M. Alcott to Her Father

Like Bunyan's pilgrim with his pack,
    Forth went the dreaming youth
To seek, to find, and make his own
    Wisdom, virtue, and truth.
Life was his book, and patiently
    He studied each hard page;
By turns reformer, outcast, priest,
    Philosopher and sage.

Christ was his Master, and he made
    His life a gospel sweet;
Plato and Pythagoras in him
    Found a disciple meet.
The noblest and best his friends,
    Faithful and fond, though few;
Eager to listen, learn, and pay
    The love and honor due.

Power and place, silver and gold,
    He neither asked nor sought;
Only to serve his fellowmen,
    With heart and word and thought.
A pilgrim still, but in his pack
    No sins to frighten or oppress;
But wisdom, morals, piety,
    To teach, to warn and bless.

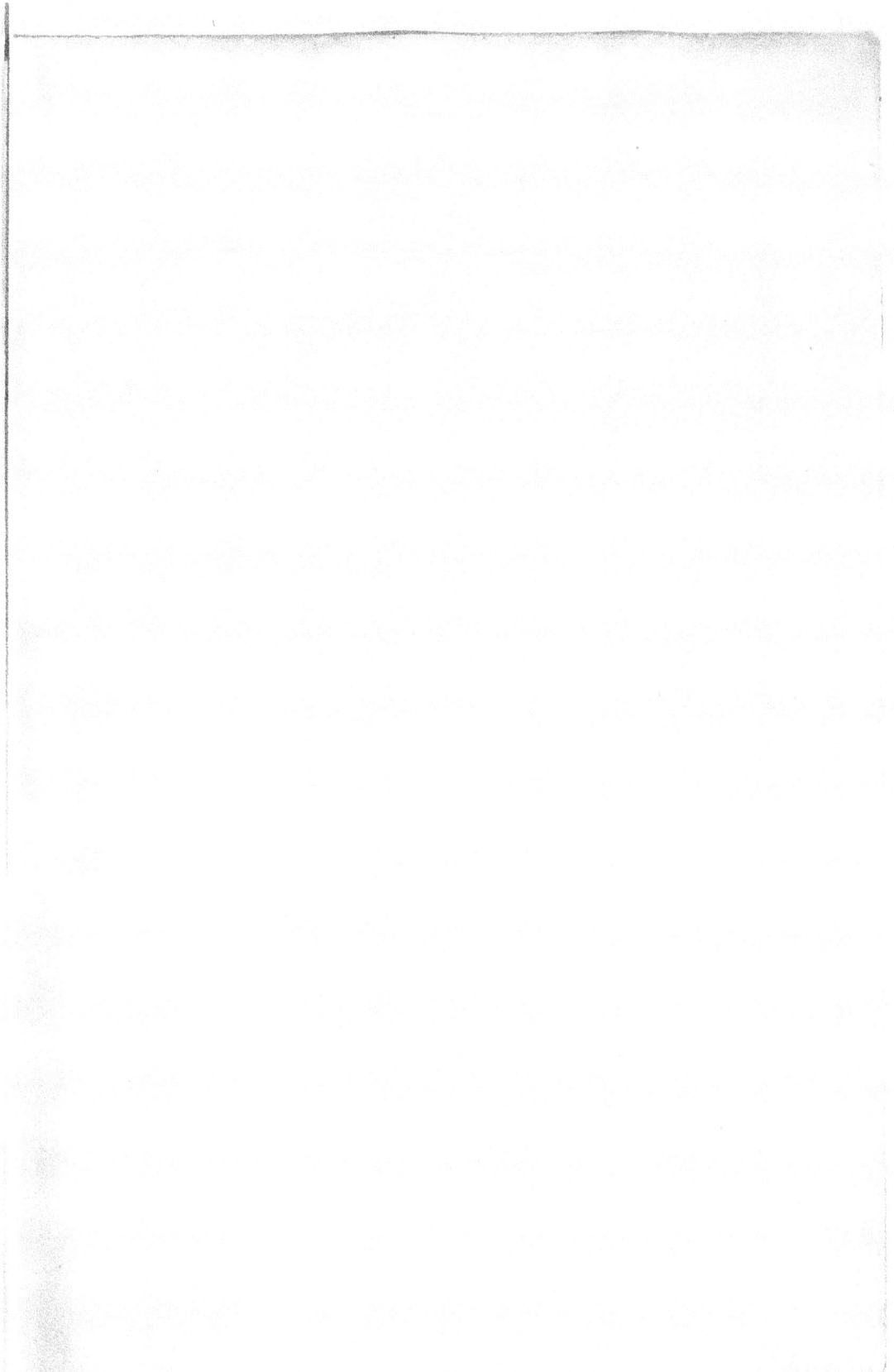

The world passed by, nor cared to take
  The treasure he could give;
Apart he sat, content to wait
  And beautifully live;
Unsaddened by long, lonely years
  Of want, neglect, and wrong,
His soul to him a kingdom was,
  Steadfast, serene, and strong.

Magnanimous and pure his life,
  Tranquil its happy end;
Patience and peace his handmaids were,
  Death an immortal friend.
For him no monuments need rise,
  No laurels make his pall;
The mem'ry of the good and wise
  Outshines, outlives them all.

The explanation of the following poem seems to give added color to it. Mr. Alcott had a habit of cutting his own hair—a feat that can certainly be called unusual!—and it was after one of these occasions that Miss Alcott picked up the curl and pasted it on the corner of the paper upon which the poem is written.

Lines Written by Louisa M. Alcott

A LITTLE GREY CURL

A little grey curl from my father's head
  I find unburned on the hearth,
And give it a place in my diary here,
  With a feeling half sadness, half mirth.
For the long white locks are our special pride,
  Though he smiles at his daughter's praise;
But, oh, they have grown each year more thin,
  Till they are now but a silvery haze.

That wise old head! (though it does grow bald
  With the knocks hard fortune may give)
Has a store of faith and hope and trust,
  Which have taught him how to live.

Thomas Todd Co. Printers

Though the hat be old, there's a face below
   Which telleth to those who look
The history of a good man's life,
   And it cheers like a blessed book.

*A peddler of jewels, of clocks, and of books,
   Many a year of his wandering youth;
A peddler still, with a far richer pack,
   His wares are wisdom and love and truth.
But now, as then, few purchase or pause,
   For he cannot learn the tricks of trade;
Little silver he wins, but that which time
   Is sprinkling thick on his meek old head.

But there'll come a day when the busy world,
   Grown sick with its folly and pride,
Will remember the mild-faced peddler then
   Whom it rudely had set aside;
Will remember the wares he offered it once
   And will seek to find him again,
Eager to purchase truth, wisdom, and love,
   But, oh, it will seek him in vain.

It will find but his footsteps left behind
   Along the byways of life,
Where he patiently walked, striving the while
   To quiet its tumult and strife.
But the peddling pilgrim has laid down his pack
   And gone with his earnings away;
How small will they seem, remembering the debt
   Which the world too late would repay.

God bless the dear head! and crown it with years
   Untroubled and calmly serene;
That the autumn of life more golden may be
   For the heats and the storms that have been.
My heritage none can ever dispute,
   My fortune will bring neither strife nor care;
'Tis an honest name, 'tis a beautiful life,
   And the silver lock of my father's hair.

*This was true of him in his early youth.

PICTURE OF "FRUITLANDS."

The old house where Bronson Alcott and the English Mystics tried to found a community somewhat after the order of Brook Farm in 1843. Emerson backed the scheme. The house is open to the public Tuesday, Thursday, and Saturday afternoons during the summer.

TO PAPA

In high Olympus' sacred shade
  A gift Minerva wrought
For her beloved philosopher
  Immersed in deepest thought.

A shield to guard his aged breast
  With its enchanted mesh
When he his nectar and ambrosia took
  To strengthen and refresh.

Long may he live to use the life
  The hidden goddess gave,
To keep unspotted to the end
  The gentle, just, and brave.

December, 1887.   LOUISA M. ALCOTT.

Before closing, another unpublished poem is added to the foregoing ones. It was written by Louise Chandler Moulton upon hearing of the death of Louisa Alcott, and is in the Fruitlands collection.

Louisa M. Alcott

IN MEMORIAM

As the wind at play with a spark
  Of fire that glows through the night;
As the speed of the soaring lark
  That wings to the sky his flight—
So swiftly thy soul has sped
  In its upward wonderful way,
Like the lark when the dawn is red,
  In search of the shining day.

Thou art not with the frozen dead
  Whom earth in the earth we lay,
While the bearers softly tread,
  And the mourners kneel and pray;
From thy semblance, dumb and stark,
  The soul has taken its flight—
Out of the finite dark,
  Into the infinite Light.

                    LOUISE CHANDLER MOULTON.

Old letters and old poems from the pen of some well-known author of the past that are found in unexpected places, or come to light through unlooked-for channels, have a special charm and flavor of their own. They seem to give out something peculiarly personal, like an echo from a voice that has long been silent.

This great devotion that Bronson Alcott inspired in those near to him is well known by those who have made a study of the remarkable group of men that formed a charmed literary circle in Concord in the middle of the last century, of whom Ralph Waldo Emerson was the distinguished leader; yet each additional proof gives an added warmth of color and a truer portrayal of the character of this quaint and original follower of the Greek philosophers and of his gifted family.

The writer of this article recalls one day when the late Frank B. Sanborn, well-known Sage of Concord, as he was called, was reading these poems at Fruitlands. When he came to the last line of the first poem herein given he dwelt upon it as if in deep thought. Then lifting his head, his face lighting with one of his sudden smiles, he murmured, "That sounds just like Louisa!"

1919   CLARA ENDICOTT SEARS.*

* Author of " Bronson Alcott's Fruitlands "; " Gleanings from Old Shaker Journals "; also a novel, " The Bell-Ringer," published by Houghton Mifflin Company, Boston, Mass. Poem, " The Unfurling of the Flag."

www.ingramcontent.com/pod-product-compliance
Lightning Source LLC
Chambersburg PA
CBHW081236020426
42331CB00012B/3202